Pet Noir

An Illustrated Anthology of
Strange but True Pet Crime Stories

Peter Conrad

Pet Noir

An Illustrated Anthology of Strange but True Pet Crime Stories

edited by
Shannon O'Leary

Manic D Press
San Francisco

Pet Noir. Copyright ©2006 by Shannon O'Leary and respective contributors. All rights reserved. Published by Manic D Press, Inc. No part of this book may be used or reproduced in any manner whatsoever without written permission from publisher except in the case of brief quotations embodied in critical articles or reviews. For information, address Manic D Press, P.O. Box 410804, San Francisco, California 94141 or www.manicdpress.com.

Printed in the United States of America.

Cover illustration: Ric Carrasquillo
Graphic design and production: Lisa Thomson

Portions of this book originally appeared in a slightly different format in a comic book edition of the same name.

Library of Congress Control Number: 2006932755
ISBN-10: 1-933149-14-0
ISBN-13: 978-1-933149-14-1

Pet Noir is dedicated to my family dog, Oscar. Thanks for all the love and fun you've given us over the years. And thanks to all the companion animals out there, for the unselfish love they give to all of us.

Shannon O'Leary

OSCAR

table of contents

Pet Noir
Notoriously strange but true tales of pet crime that made sensational headlines.

table of contents

Pet Crime Confidential
Hair-raising personal stories of everyday crimes against animals.

Welcome to **Pet Noir**

An introduction by Shannon O'Leary with images by Ric Carrasquillo

Did you hear about that blind man?
The one in Scotland?

Did you hear about how he bit his own guide dog?

Then there was the rumor about the huge international singer superstar.

No, not that "other" rumor.

It's also been said that he touched his monkey inappropriately.

He said he was just changing its diaper.

And then there was the one about the guy with the kittens.

He duct-taped their legs together so he could feed them to his pet python.

He was tired of buying his snake food.

But a blind man biting a guide dog, a pop star molesting his monkey, and a guy feeding kittens to his python are only rumors about animals and what people can do to them.

Prepare to go beyond urban myth and speculation! Reader, please beware that what follows are strange, shocking, and indisputably true tales of pet crime...

Marilyn arrived at the house at 7:00 AM sharp for feeding time.

It wasn't the first time Marilyn's cat obsession had gotten out of hand. In 1994, she was sued by her former landlords for $75,000 worth of damage caused by over 50 cats.

She was arrested on the spot and charged with animal cruelty.

There was even a case in the '70s where the owners of a Sebastopol unit sued her for $7,000 worth of damage, allegedly caused by her cats.

Hoarding animals knows no reason. One woman kept pigs in her LA home.

A woman in Connecticut hoarded beavers she had shipped to her home from Montana.

In May of 2002, Marilyn hadn't ever been to court yet and she was caught with 40 more cats in a 1 X 20 foot office in Sausalito.

Someone has stolen my cats!

She really couldn't help herself. She called the cops when the cats went missing.

Ironically, her landlord was a veterinarian. After entering the premises to investigate an all too familiar stench of urine and feces, he had the cats sent to animal rescue.

FLUFFY

Paul Musso

Lady! What tha f**kin´ f**k is WRONG with you!!!

Oh my goodness, I am so sorry. But you came out of nowhere and I didn't see you. I just...

ARP.

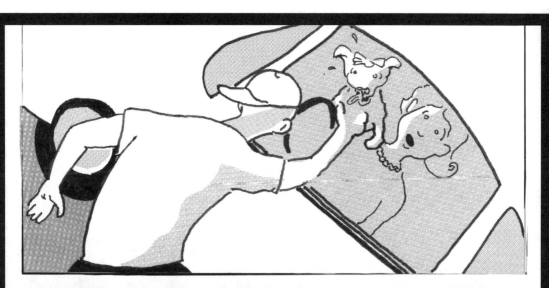

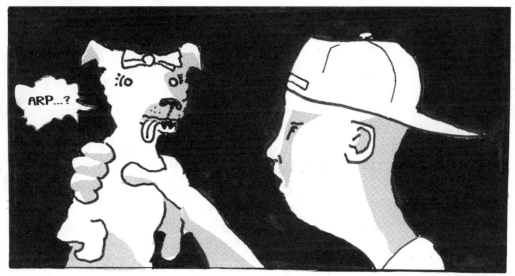

Sara rushed Leo to a veterinary hospital, but he could not be saved.

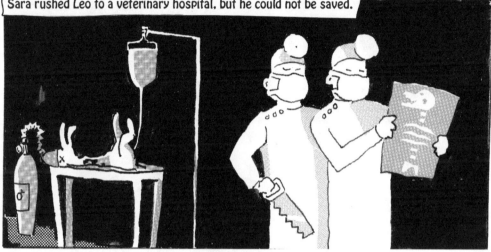

After Leo's untimely death, Sara's heart was broken.

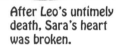

The case touched a nerve with the pet-loving public. There was huge international media interest.

McBurnett became the darling of the talk show circuit.

The assailant was dubbed "the most hated man in America".

WANTED DOG THROWER

Donations to the reward for his capture eventually reached $120,000.

Finally there was a break in the case. An anonymous source implicated Andrew Burnett. Subsequent surveillance photography determined Burnett owned a black SUV.

And that the SUV had damning Virginia license plates.

Burnett was already in jail when he got busted for Leo's murder. He was indicted on felony animal cruelty charges in April, 2001. The trial proved to be as dramatic as little Leo's passing.

His clear intent was to terrorize me in the fastest and severest way he would under the circumstances.

Burnett claimed that he instinctively snatched Leo from the car and threw him into oncoming traffic after Leo viciously attacked him.

He tried to be remorseful.

I am really sorry for what happened. If there is anything I could ever say or do to bring Leo back, I would.

THE CHRISTMAS KOALA CAPER

SF ZOO

It was Christmas Night of the year 2000 and at the San Francisco Zoo, not a creature was stirring...

Not a howl could be heard from the Black Howler Monkeys

The Giraffes were as tall and still as trees

The Flamingos were as motionless as lawn ornaments.

WORDS: O'LEARY
IMAGES HEWICKER

KOALA CROSSING

STEP... STEP. STEP. STEP.

aaack!

But, there were strange goings on at the zoo's popular Koala Crossing exhibit. And on the day after Christmas, two of the koalas were MISSING.

WHERE COULD THEY HAVE GONE TO?

It was the year 2000 and things were changing fast. Fear and uncertainty were in the air and exotic zoo animals were not immune to it. Did they give in to visions of an impending Armageddon and join a new millennium cult? Were they waiting for the end times somewhere?

THE END IS NEAR

CUT!

Z-Z-Z

Perhaps it was more benign. Maybe they went off to find fame as Ewok extras in the new Star Wars prequel.

Or maybe they went to seek their fortune. Perhaps they became e-commerce millionaires in the internet gold rush.

KOALA.COM, HUH? I LIKE IT BUT WHAT DOES IT DO?

Where could they have gone? They had been stolen from the zoo sometime after 6 PM on Christmas day, most likely by someone seeking an exotic pet. Such thefts have become the norm, with several of the animals never being recovered.

MISSING SINCE 2000

2 TAMARIND MONKEYS MICKE GROVE ZOO, LODI

3 EAGLES SANTA BARBARA ZOO

OTTER OAKLAND ZOO

LEANNE

PAT

The two missing koalas were a mother and daughter named Pat and Leanne. They had been raised in captivity. Since koalas are considered an endangered species, police and FBI agents alerted officials at border crossings and major airports to be on the lookout. A nationwide manhunt for the thieves was underway.

THÚ VÂT Ở NGOÀI!

It would turn out that they were at an elderly Buddhist, Vietnamese non-English-speaking couple's house in Visitacion Valley. Of all the places the koalas could have gone to, how'd they get there???

We wish we could tell you they had a nice stay there, but unfortunately they didn't. Koalas don't like being around people much. They may be very cute, but they're not very affectionate.

It would be nice to say they were sampling exotic cuisines of the Far East, but koalas are very finicky eaters. They only eat one type of eucalyptus leaf and that's ALL they eat.

To say that Pat and Leanne didn't like it there at all is putting it mildly. They were found in the hallway of the house, which was littered with their droppings. They were terrorized and dehydrated but otherwise unharmed. Police found the koalas after responding to an anonymous tip from a concerned citizen. At approximately 2:30 AM they surrounded the house and spotted the two cute environmentally sensitive animals through a window.

NGOÀI! HO HOI!!

The suspect was the 17-year-old son of the couple. His parents were not aware that the critters had been stolen and were becoming very annoyed with them. His father told police through an interpreter that he was going to wait one more day and let the koalas go because they were beginning to irritate him.

The juvenile suspect matched a composite drawing of a suspicious acting man seen asking questions of the koala keeper on Christmas day.

She later heard loud noises on the roof of the Koala Crossing exhibit and saw a man's hand on the skylight.

After security guards arrived, they questioned a second suspicious-looking boy scoping out the exhibit. He claimed to have followed a peacock into the area.

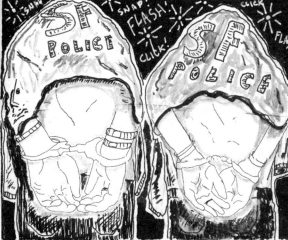

The second boy turned out to be a 15-year-old friend of the first boy. They told police they hopped a fence to get in the zoo, made off with the koalas wrapped in a blanket, then hopped back over the fence.

They were apprehended and remanded to juvenile hall under charges of burglary, grand theft and stolen property.

The motive of the crime was affection. The two boys had stolen the koalas to give to their girl-friends as belated Christmas presents. The plan went awry when the girls rejected the gifts and the youths were stuck with the koalas.

All's well that ends well. The two boys were convicted as juveniles and sentenced to eight years. The SF Zoo made efforts to increase security and prevent further thefts. Pat and Leanne were returned to their home, none the worse for wear, putting an end to the Koala Christmas Caper.

Mary Fleener

Melanie Lewis

Some people have the best intentions.

Others, they've only got their own interests at heart.

And some, they got no heart at all. Either way the road to Hell ain't pavin' itself.

Case in point: Mister John Weinhart. He seemed like your typical do-gooder. Him and his wife, Marla Smith, ran an animal sanctuary down in SoCal, a place for circus and entertainment industry cats to go to when their gig was up.

Some say Weinhart was a man with a "feel" for large cats, who got along better with animals than he did with people. In fact, Weinhart himself was known to say exactly that...

Weinhart's stint with animals started in the 1960s, with a pet shop in Inglewood, California.

In the '70s, in LA, the city of angels, he and his ol' lady, Marla Smith, ran a nightclub act.

Weinhart became known as a breeder and peddler of leopards and sumatran tigers. He worked circuses.

He worked shopping malls.

He starred his animals in movies.

He tried to break into Vegas by renting his cats out to magic acts.

Eventually, the acts gave way to selling animals.

And any other money-making endeavor he could think up.

Weinhart claimed he got the bright idea for Tiger Rescue after coming across stacks of tiger skulls in 'Nam.

Weinhart based this operation at his house in Glen Avon until '98, when a zoning law forced him to move it to a former sewage plant in nearby Colton. The grounds became a popular weekend destination for local residents.

Weinhart was a local hero. But things aren't always as they seem. From the get-go, the State Department of Fish and Game got all sorts of complaints about Tiger Rescue and cited them several times for crummy conditions.

✻The Roar Foundation and Shambala Preserve are Tippi Hedren's exotic animal rescue services.

The animals lived in their own waste and did not have enough to drink because the only water was placed in upside-down trash lids!

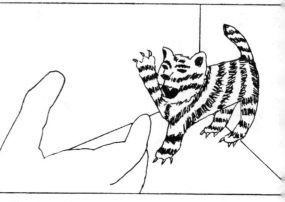

Tippi Hedren, the former Hitchcock blonde, who ran a wildlife sanctuary in Acton, California, paid a visit to Tiger Rescue and was put off by its skuzzy conditions. She dropped a dime to the U.S. Department of Agriculture to complain.

In November 2002, the Department of Fish and Game raided the Colton facility after getting a tip that a tiger cub might be living there. Ten tigers were seized and Weinhart was nailed on a bunch of misdemeanors.

In 2003, Weinhart's home in Glen Avon was raided again. John Weinhart and Marla Smith were charged with 16 felony counts of animal cruelty. Authorities found 13 young tigers and 2 adults who were later rubbed out.

Weinhart and Smith were also hit with one count of child endangerment, presumably for the two alligators they found in the bathtub.

The animal cruelty counts were based on the pathetic living conditions of the animals and included breeding without a permit, squalid cages, and not enough food and water. The violations were NOT based on the discovery of 90 tiger stiffs, including 58 cubs found stuffed in freezers and adults found rotting on their property. Weinhart said he was preserving the decomposing tigers' bones and pelts for later sales and claimed he froze the dead cubs for a pending postmortem exam to determine how they died.

Marla Smith pled guilty in a plea bargain to one felony count of willful cruelty to a child, 16 felony counts of animal cruelty, and 46 misdemeanor violations involving the care of the animals.

John Weinhart was sentenced to two years under glass and five years of probation.

But not everybody thought Weinhart was a bad guy...

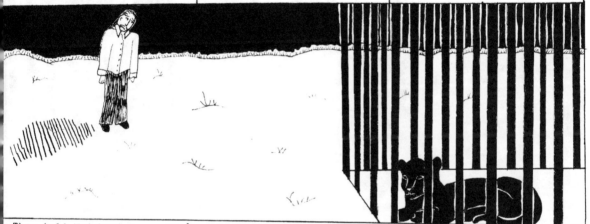

They told Weinhart he couldn't own, possess, care for, or volunteer in a place with animals. He was also told to stay fifty yards away from exotic cats.

Did Weinhart have good intentions?   Or was he just a bad seed?

Does it really matter?

THE SAGA OF SPIKE THE CAT

What follows is the heart-wrenching saga of Spike the Cat. Names and identifying details in this story have been changed to protect the innocent, just and noble.

"Dear Lord,
please help me score 3
Match points for a successful flag hang.
I am not asking a whole lot, Lord.
I just want to do real good at paint ball
and lead my teammates to victory in
your name. That's not really asking
a lot, is it, Lord?"

story: Shannon O'Leary

art: Andy Ristaino

Later that day...

He's not my cat. I just take care of him. The old man who lives here - I take care of all his cats.

...How did you know the cat was dead?

He got hit by a car. The cat.

I remember that cat. That cat chased my dog and he ran away.

Lillian loved Spike, the cat she found dead in the alley, dearly.

He never came back.

It struck her as odd that Henry would blame the loss of his dog on Spike.

She tried to put it out of her head but it didn't make sense to her that Spike had been hit by a car. He had always stayed clear of the street.

She buried him in the old man's yard but as the days went by, she had a hunch she just couldn't shake.

So she exhumed Spike's body and took him to the vet for an autopsy where an x-ray revealed a gun pellet at the base of his skull.

She remembered seeing Henry shooting at birds with a bb gun and it all came together.

That cat made my dog run away. He ran away and never came back.

Finally, Lilian had to make peace with herself and called the police. They said they wouldn't come unless the crime was on videotape but Lillian persisted.

Henry confessed immediately after being confronted by the investigating officer. His motive was one of revenge.

I'm sorry. I didn't know that was your cat.

I don't want to talk to you. You did a horrible thing.

After he confessed, he asked to talk to Lillian. She had nothing to say to him. She would later describe him as a "lost boy" and a loser. Although this was the first time Henry had been in trouble with the law, it was not the first time his behavior had raised eyebrows.

You're supposed to be doing re-con, not offense!

Yeah, sissy! Go ahead and cry outta your right eye, you non fully functioning left eye, wuss!

It had been "eating him up inside" that he couldn't play paintball due to an injury that had sidelined him. Neighbors reported that he would take this out in bizarre ways.

He had dropped out of high school to join the Navy Seals but was not accepted because he had had surgery in his left eye.

She contacted the Animal Legal Defense Fund who took on the case, testified for the prosecution, wrote a letter to the judge and attended the trial daily.

In early 2004, Henry was convicted on one count of misdemeanor cruelty to animals. He was sentenced to 3 years probation, a $500 fine, 45 days of public work and anger management counseling.

Professionals estimated Henry got off easy because his father spent upwards of $10,000 on attorney fees and a psych evaluation.

Henry's family no longer lives next to the old man. He is rumored to be working in India as a missionary for a non-denominational Christian church.

Lillian continues to battle for the rights of the underdog. She recently fought to get a homeless man in her neighborhood social security benefits. If those who hear Spike's story could learn anything from it, Lillian would like for people to view humans and animals as equals. She had Spike cremated and keeps his remains with her at home.

THE CASE OF THE SAN FRANCISCO

DOG MAULING

AAAIGHHH!

Growl
Wait.
No!

Wh-who's there?

WRITTEN BY: SHANNON O'LEARY   ART BY: MARINAOMI

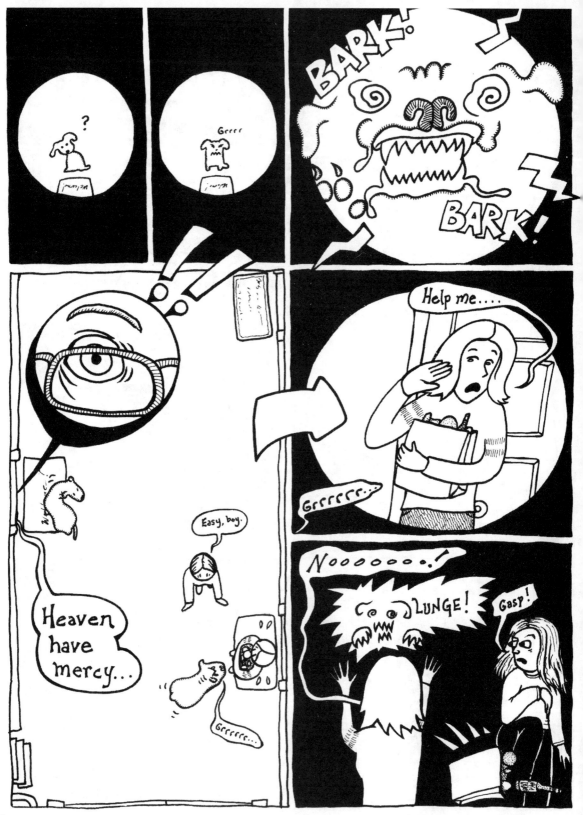

WHAT HAPPENED WAS PRETTY SIMPLE. A YOUNG WOMAN WAS MAULED TO DEATH BY ONE, POSSIBLY TWO, VERY BAD DOGS IN ONE OF SAN FRANCISCO'S MOST AFFLUENT NEIGHBORHOODS. DIANE WHIPPLE DIED THE MORNING AFTER SHE WAS ATTACKED. BANE, THE MALE DOG WHO FATALLY BIT HER ON THE NECK, WAS PUT TO SLEEP THE NIGHT OF THE INCIDENT BY ORDER OF THE SAN FRANCISCO ANIMAL CARE AND CONTROL (ACC) DEPARTMENT. HERA, THE FEMALE DOG WHO MAY HAVE TAKEN PART IN THE KILLING, WAS TAKEN INTO ACC CUSTODY.

WHAT CAME BEFORE THAT, WHAT HAPPENED AFTERWARDS AND WHO WAS RESPONSIBLE FOR THIS TRAGEDY IS NOWHERE NEAR AS STRAIGHTFORWARD.

ALTHOUGH THE ATTACK TOOK PLACE IN A HIGH SOCIETY SAN FRANCISCO NEIGHBORHOOD, THE STORY BEGAN AT THE NOTORIOUS PELICAN BAY SUPERMAX PRISON WHERE PAUL SCHNEIDER, A TOP OPERATIVE IN THE ARYAN BROTHERHOOD (AB), A WHITE SUPREMACIST GANG, WAS SERVING A LIFE SENTENCE WITHOUT PAROLE.

PAUL SCHNEIDER HAD A WAY WITH WOMEN. ONE WOMAN MOVED FROM CRESCENT CITY TO SACRAMENTO JUST TO BE NEAR HIM. SHE GAVE HIM MONEY. SHE SMUGGLED DRUGS INTO THE JOINT FOR HIM. SHE EVEN MASTERMINDED AN ELABORATE JAILBREAK TO BUST HIM OUT.

THE ESCAPE PLAN FAILED AND SCHNEIDER'S OLD LADY WAS LOCKED UP AS A RESULT. AFTER SHE WAS INCARCERATED, SCHNEIDER NEEDED DRUGS AND MONEY. HE CAME UP WITH A SCHEME TO BREED PRESA CANARIO DOGS AND SELL THEM TO GUARD MEXICAN MAFIA DRUG LABS.

SCHNEIDER AND HIS CELLMATE MASTERMINDED THE WHOLE SCHEME FROM THE INSIDE. THEY WORKED WITH AB CONTACTS ON THE OUTSIDE TO PURCHASE THE DOGS. THEN, ONE OF THE AB MEMBERS CONVINCED A NAÏVE CHRISTIAN WOMAN WHO LIVED ON A SMALL FARM THAT SCHNEIDER NEEDED SAVING.

AFTER INTIMATE CORRESPONDENCE AND PRISON VISITS, SCHNEIDER CONVINCED HER SHE NEEDED GUARD DOGS FOR PROTECTION, FUN AND PROFIT.

SCHNEIDER AND HIS GIRLFRIEND HAD A FALLING OUT AND HE CALLED ON JAILHOUSE LAWYERS ROBERT NOEL AND MARJORIE KNOLLER TO GET HIS DOGS BACK. NOEL AND KNOLLER WERE PARTNERS IN LAW AND MARRIAGE. THEY HAD FILED A TOTAL OF 150 LAWSUITS AGAINST THE CALIFORNIA DEPARTMENT OF CORRECTIONS.

NOEL AND KNOLLER FELL IN LOVE WITH BANE AND HERA. THEY ADOPTED THEM AND SENT THE REMAINING PRESAS TO AN AB ASSOCIATE IN LA. THE DOGS, WHO HAD BEEN DIFFICULT TO MANAGE ON A SMALL FARM, GOT COMPLETELY OUT OF CONTROL IN THE LAWYERS' ONE BEDROOM APARTMENT. NEIGHBORS IN THE BUILDING FEARED THEM.

This is an order to remove these dogs from your premises

Ask not for whom the dog barks.

It barks for thee.

NOEL AND KNOLLER'S INVOLVEMENT WITH SCHNEIDER EVOLVED WAY BEYOND A TRADITIONAL ATTORNEY/CLIENT RELATIONSHIP. THEY REFERRED TO THEMSELVES AS "THE TRIAD" OR THE "FAMILY OF THREE". SCHNEIDER DETAILED THEIR MAGICAL, MEDIEVAL ARYAN FANTASY WORLD IN A SERIES OF SEXUALLY CHARGED DRAWINGS THAT INCLUDED THE DOGS.

HERA
ONE RED-HOT BITCH

THE QUEEN

THE KING

THE PRINCE

THE BANESTER

THIS ARRANGEMENT WOULD LATER MOVE BEYOND MERE FANTASY TO A BINDING AND LEGAL AGREEMENT. WITHIN DAYS OF DIANE WHIPPLE'S DEATH, NOEL AND KNOLLER LEGALLY ADOPTED PAUL SCHNEIDER.

I'm so proud of our Aryan, sociopath, murdering, canine-loving son!

THERE WERE RUMORS THAT POLICE FOUND PHOTOGRAPHIC EVIDENCE OF NOEL AND KNOLLER ENGAGING IN BESTIALITY WITH THE DOGS.

THE BESTIALITY RUMORS WERE NEVER PROVEN TRUE OR FALSE, BUT NOEL AND KNOLLER WERE PERCEIVED AS TOTAL WEIRDOS NONETHELESS, AND THAT PERCEPTION STUCK. WHEN NOEL IMPLIED THE ATTACK WAS WHIPPLE'S FAULT BECAUSE THE DOGS WERE SEXUALLY ATTRACTED TO HER SCENT, THE LAWYERS BECAME HEARTLESS IN THE PUBLIC'S EYES, AS WELL.

WHEN THEY DEMANDED A HEARING TO SAVE HERA'S LIFE, IT CAME OFF AS ARROGANT AND INSENSITIVE. PUBLIC OUTRAGE ENSUED.

THE ACC RECEIVED THREATENING CALLS FROM BOTH SYMPATHETIC DOG OWNERS SAYING HERA'S LIFE SHOULD BE SPARED AND CITIZENS CONCERNED FOR THEIR SAFETY, INSISTING SHE BE TERMINATED IMMEDIATELY. MEDIA COVERAGE OF THE HEARING WAS EXTENSIVE. A WIDESPREAD FEAR OF BIG DOGS HIT THE STREETS. DAY AFTER DAY, THE PUBLIC HEARD HOW BANE AND HERA TERRORIZED THEIR PACIFIC HEIGHTS NEIGHBORHOOD AND HOW NOEL AND KNOLLER COULD NOT CONTROL THEM. IN FACT, OTHER DOG OWNERS SAID THEY DID NOT TRY TO.

THE DOGS LUNGED AT CHILDREN...

AND PREGNANT WOMEN.

THE ACC JUDGE ORDERED THAT HERA BE DESTROYED, BUT THE DA'S OFFICE REQUESTED THAT SHE BE HELD AS POTENTIAL EVIDENCE AT AN ANIMAL SHELTER UNTIL CRIMINAL CHARGES WERE FILED AGAINST NOEL AND KNOLLER.

FROM THERE, THINGS ONLY GOT MORE SURREAL AND SENSATIONAL AS THE MEDIA CONCERNED ITSELF WITH THE TWISTS, TURNS, QUIRKS AND PECCADILLOS OF THE PEOPLE INVOLVED IN THE CASE...

SHARON SMITH, DIANE WHIPPLE'S PARTNER, BECAME A GAY ACTIVIST OVERNIGHT WHEN SHE BROUGHT A WRONGFUL DEATH SUIT AGAINST NOEL AND KNOLLER. IF SHE WON, EVERY GAY MAN AND WOMAN IN AMERICA COULD POTENTIALLY GAIN STATUS AS A RECOGNIZED PARTNER WITH SPOUSAL RIGHTS.

> Any settlement I receive will go to the Diane Whipple Foundation to fund female lacrosse players.

GAY ACTIVIST

MEANWHILE, SCHNEIDER'S DOG-O-WAR OPERATION WAS ALIVE AND WELL. THE OFFSPRING OF BANE AND ISIS WERE BREEDING IN SOUTHERN CALIFORNIA. ONE OF THE PUPS WAS NAMED "MENACE". HIS OWNER RAN ADS SAYING THAT BANE HAD SIRED THE PUPS AND CITED THE SAN FRANCISCO DOG MAULING AS EVIDENCE OF THEIR ATTACK DOG PROWESS.

PHOTOGENIC PROSECUTOR KIMBERLY GUILFOYLE WAS INITIALLY ASSIGNED THE CRIMINAL CASE AGAINST NOEL AND KNOLLER BUT QUIT AFTER SHE BECAME ENGAGED TO FUTURE SF MAYOR GAVIN NEWSOM. SHE RECEIVED A DEATH THREAT FROM PAUL SCHNEIDER AND ENDED UP WEARING A BULLET-PROOF VEST TO HER OWN REHEARSAL DINNER.

THE DEATH THREAT LATER TURNED OUT TO BE A FAKE, BUT GUILFOYLE'S PRECAUTIONARY MEASURE WAS INDICATIVE OF THE FEAR IN SAN FRANCISCO AT THE TIME. THIS WAS DUE IN LARGE PART TO THE MEDIA COVERAGE, WHICH WAS SO RELENTLESS THAT THE TRIAL HAD TO BE MOVED TO LOS ANGELES.

> ?
> Honey, does this bullet-proof vest make me look fat?

ACME

← SHINY!

KRON

> This is COURT TV interrupting our LIVE, gavel-to-gavel coverage of the San Francisco DOG MAULING trial to bring you the important announcement that even though the trial is being moved to LA because there will be less paparazzi there, we will continue to be there for EVERY STEP..........

NOEL AND KNOLLER WERE CHARGED WITH NU-
MEROUS VICIOUS DOG VIOLATIONS — AND KNOL-
LER WITH 2ND DEGREE MURDER. MUCH ADO
WAS MADE IN THE PRESS ABOUT KNOLLER'S
ATTORNEY, NEDRA RUIZ, WHO ADVOCATED FOR
HER CLIENT IN A MANNER THAT COULD ONLY BE
DESCRIBED AS BIZARRE AND, AT TIMES, DEFAMA-
TORY. AT ONE POINT SHE GOT DOWN ON ALL FOURS
TO RE-ENACT HER CLIENT'S ATTEMPT TO SAVE
DIANE WHIPPLE'S LIFE.

KNOLLER TESTIFIED THAT SHE FOUGHT
VALIANTLY TO SAVE WHIPPLE'S LIFE. UN-
FORTUNATELY, ACCORDING TO KNOLLER, WHIP-
PLE MADE IT WORSE BY TRYING TO FIGHT BACK.

HELLLP MEEE!!!

You know, all that flailing your arms around and hitting my dog doesn't seem to be helping.

Like this: "woof!"

MARJORIE KNOLLER AND ROBERT NOEL WERE BOTH SENTENCED TO FOUR YEARS IN
PRISON. NOEL WAS RELEASED ON SEPTEMBER 15, 2003. KNOLLER'S 2ND DEGREE MUR-
DER CONVICTION WAS THROWN OUT WHEN A CALIFORNIA SUPREME COURT JUDGE
DEEMED NOEL AND KNOLLER WOULD HAVE NO WAY OF KNOWING WHEN THEIR DOGS
WOULD ATTACK TO KILL. SHE WAS PAROLED JANUARY 2, 2004. IT IS RUMORED THEIR
MARRIAGE TOOK A TURN FOR THE WORSE AS A RESULT OF THE TRIAL.

You are the most despised couple in the city. I don't think anybody likes you!

JUDGE NOT LEST YE BE JUDGED

EVENTUALLY, HERA WAS EXTERMINATED, JUST LIKE BANE. SHE WENT CRAZY
DURING HER TIME AS EVIDENCE, ALONE IN A SMALL CAGE AND NOT ALLOWED
TO GO OUTSIDE FOR OVER A YEAR IN ACC CUSTODY. HER ASHES WERE GIVEN TO
AN ANIMAL RIGHTS ACTIVIST WHO FOUGHT TO SAVE HER.

Owrooooo...

THE END

When the ambulance arrived, Brian Loudermilk was still alive but fading in and out of consciousness. As the EMT's eased the SUV off of him, they saw that he had been lying in a shallow ditch. The car's tire was sitting on a board and pillow which appeared to cushion him from the crushing weight of the vehicle.

He died shortly after arriving at the hospital but his startling tale of peculiar sexual depravity and the subculture that catered to it had just begun.

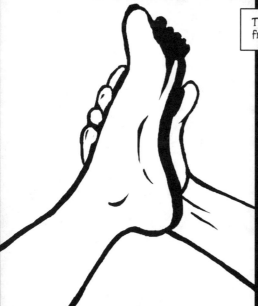

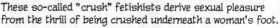
These so-called "crush" fetishists derive sexual pleasure from the thrill of being crushed underneath a woman's foot.

Brian Loudermilk was part of a fringe subset of foot fetishists who aren't just into playing footsies.

Loudermilk even designed a special prosthetic leg to keep him company when his wife was unavailable. It was a wooden foot outfitted with spikes on the bottom that sometimes left scars on his chest.

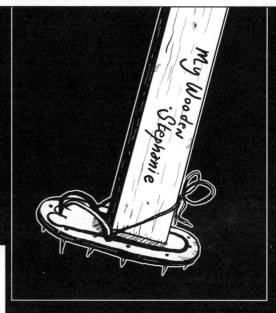

And not just any woman's foot. Crush fetishists like large women with large feet that crush hard. Loudermilk himself often fantasized about giant women trampling entire villages. A vision he sketched and shared with other Crush enthusiasts.

He also sought the company of women outside of his marriage and was known to pay up to $50.00 an hour for "foot goddesses" to walk on him.

what you want. I can be dominant or submissive. Be clean. No diseases, play safe. ☎41562

Generous 26 yo male w/ appetite for female feet. I LOVE FEET! Being walked on, suck toes, licking feet, or crush, I love all aspects of feet. ✉62489

I am seeking a mature dad for father and son fantasy play. I am a straight,

6, 125#, green respond if you ave my ways to

t a fantasy of mouth The will and i will flow ill clean

most is a bad

Pretty much everyone knew about Brian Loudermilk's strange proclivities – even his mom.

He told me that he had a fetish for, like, feet. I figured, well, that's his thing

But he wasn't just into getting his own crush on – he got off on the thrill of the crush itself. He engaged in the most controversial form of crush there is – that of living creatures like insects...

...And small animals.

Steph cruel. See the little chicken? SQUASH.

Then he videotaped it. Several videos of Stephanie Loudermilk stepping on rabbits, birds, goldfish and mice until they died were discovered after his death.

The Loudermilks actually owned a mom and pop fetish production company called B&S Foot Action that employed several women and specialized in "videos, photos, and arts of female feet in action" – crushing and trampling.

At the time of Loudermilk's death there was a nationwide law enforcement crackdown on crush videos and celebrity animal activists like Mickey Rooney and M*A*S*H's Loretta Switt were demanding legislation that would outlaw them.

Regardless, President Bill Clinton signed a bill into law in 1999 that made selling videos depicting animal torture a federal crime punishable by up to 5 years in prison.

Crush videos are still being offered by clandestine websites in Amsterdam and China but they quickly vanish when they attract too much attention and inflame public outrage.

In 2000, Stephanie Loudermilk was convicted on two counts of animal cruelty. She served no time and claimed her late husband beat her participation out of her.

Although Brian Loudermilk's murder was never officially solved his spirit lives on. In 1999, he was nominated for a Darwin award, an honor given to those who "improve the human genome by removing themselves from it."

Welcome to

Pet Crime

An introduction by Shannon O'Leary with images by Ric Carrasquillo

It has been said that there are a million stories in the naked city.

"Buckle up, Fido, you're comin' with us

But not every family dog that gets stolen by a biker gang finds its way into a police report.

And when a boy grudgingly agrees to mow the lawn and discovers mice nesting in the motor of the lawnmower, the ensuing mayhem doesn't usually wind up on the front page of a major newspaper.

And the life story of every cat that runs away from home for the better part of a year only to return and lose a leg falling out of a tree does not generally find itself under the glaring scrutiny of the public eye.

Like most stories of the urban jungle, those tales will remain untold. What follows, however, are five up-close and personal, 100% true tales of animal injustice for your perusal. Read these riveting Pet Noir accounts of Pet Crime CONFIDENTIAL with care...

GRAY GHOST (PART II) (SORT OF)

MELANIE LEWIS

In 1985, we (my brother Cam, my mom, my dad, Mosby the Schnoodle & I) went on a family vacation to Florida. We got in pretty late.

Everyone was tired, so my parents decided to stay in Miami for the night and head to our final destination in the morning.

JUST LEAVE THAT ONE IN THE CAR, BOB.

No pets were allowed at the motel, so Mosby had to sleep in the car.

We woke up early to an unfortunate development.

(tellin' it like it is)

WAKE UP, MEL. CAR'S BEEN STOLEN. MOSBY'S GONE.

HUH?

We never saw him again. It was sad for us.

BUT HEY! That doesn't mean it was sad for Mosby. You know: One door shuts, another opens!

POLICE

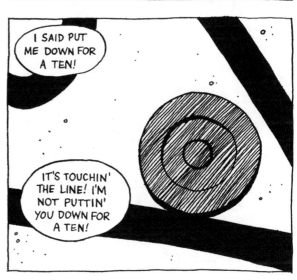

It's tough to make it on your own, though. Especially after a lifetime of not having to.

SO THIS IS JUST A BASIC EXCEL APTITUDE TEST. A LOT OF OUR CLIENTS WANT TO MAKE SURE THE TEMPS KNOW THEIR WAY AROUND A SPREADSHEET.

TAP TAP

MY NAME'S MARY-JO, JUST COME GET ME IF YOU HAVE ANY QUESTIONS.

Select cell A2.

CLICK

Your score: 12% CORRECT!

HEY, MARY-JO, I JUST REALIZED I LEFT MY GLASSES IN THE CAR, SO I'M JUST GONNA RUN OUT AND GET THEM AND I'LL BE RIGHT BACK TO FINISH UP THE TEST.

Your score: 12% CORRECT!

SEE YOU IN A FEW, MOSBY.

YEP.

SOB SOB

I'm pretty sure this didn't happen, though. This was, after all, 1985.

My mom has this habit of labeling perfectly recognizable photographs with a ballpoint pen directly on the image.

My strongest memory of Mosby is actually just a photograph. He's lying down on a crocheted bedspread and the sunlight's shining on him so he looks really angelic. Fortunately, my mom has scrawled "Mosby" across it, so we all know it's definitely him.

(the first ballpoint pen didn't work)

For no apparent reason, my mom most often suggests that Mosby was eaten by Cubans whenever the topic of his fate comes up.

By settling on such an unlikely and extreme possibility, I think she's able to avoid the reality of how tragic the event was. I have to admit that I feel a little sick when I dwell on what really might have happened.

I recently found out that Mosby's namesake, Confederate partisan ranger John Singleton Mosby, was nicknamed the "Gray Ghost" for his ability to evade the Union army by blending in with local residents.

It doesn't seem so unreasonable to think that our Mosby might have evaded us the same way. Does it?

ES TODO.

Satan is in your Cat

A FED BEAR IS A DEAD BEAR

IN THE 1950'S PEOPLE FED BEARS GARBAGE FOR ENTERTAINMENT AT NATIONAL PARKS.

John Isaacson

BUT ONCE THE BEARS WERE HOOKED ON HUMAN FOOD, THEY BEGAN BREAKING INTO CARS, CAMPSITES, AND CABINS.

GROUNDSKEEPERS STARTED SPRAYING TRASH CAN LIDS WITH AMMONIA TO KEEP THE BEARS AWAY.

BUT MANY OF THE BEARS PERSISTED

THEY BECAME "PROBLEM BEARS" AND HAD TO BE KILLED.

FOR YEARS MY FAMILY CAMPED AT FALLEN LEAF LAKE NEAR LAKE TAHOE IN THE DESOLATION WILDERNESS AREA WHERE THERE'S BEEN A DROUGHT FOR THE PAST SEVEN YEARS.

ONCE, TWO BEARS, DRIVEN BY DROUGHT, SHOWED UP AT OUR CAMP.

THE CAMPERS WERE EITHER EAGER TO SEE THE BEARS OR TERRIFIED OF THEM.

BUT THE BEARS MOVED TOO QUICKLY TO BE SEEN FOR VERY LONG.

ON ANOTHER OCCASION, MY GRANDMOTHER AND AUNT WERE ASLEEP IN THEIR CABIN ON THE LAKE...

WHEN ALL OF A SUDDEN, THEY HEARD A SCRATCHING, RIPPING, AND TEARING SOUND.

SOMETHING WAS IN THE PANTRY!!!

CRASH

THE NEXT DAY MY GRANDFATHER ORDERED A BEAR TRAP.

THE FOREST SERVICE INSTALLED A CULVERT TRAP IN THE PARKING LOT.

IF A BEAR WAS CAUGHT IN THE TRAP, IT WOULD BE TRANQUILIZED AND RELOCATED.

SOMEONE LEFT A NOTE IN THE TRAP SUGGESTING MY ENTIRE FAMILY BE TRANQUILIZED AND RELOCATED.

AFTER SITTING IN THE PARKING LOT FOR THE ENTIRE SUMMER WITHOUT INCIDENT, THE TRAP WAS FINALLY REMOVED.

LATER THAT SUMMER, MY SISTER WAS SITTING IN THE FAMILY VAN WHEN IT BEGAN SHAKING VIOLENTLY.

WHEN SHE LOOKED UP, SHE WAS FACE-TO-FACE WITH A BEAR!

SHE TRIED TO TAKE A PHOTO BUT BY THE TIME SHE GOT HER CAMERA OUT, THE BEAR WAS GONE.

WE EVENTUALLY VISITED THE SITE WHERE PROBLEM BEARS WERE RELOCATED IN SOUTHERN ARIZONA.

AS WE GAZED OUT AT THE BARREN HORIZON, WE WONDERED...

... HOW COULD ANY BEAR SURVIVE OUT THERE?

COUGARNURSING 101
BY ALIXOPULOS

SARA HAD WORKED MANY YEARS AS A NURSE AT SAN QUENTIN PRISON. SUCH WORK HAD LEFT HER WITH A DIM VIEW OF HER FELLOW HUMANS.

SHE REMOVED HERSELF TO AN ISOLATED RURAL COMMUNITY. THERE, HER INTER-ACTIONS WITH HER NEIGHBORS WERE LIMITED TO OCCASIONAL HOSTILE SHOUTS AND GESTURES.

SLOW DOWN!!

CAMARO

NO TRESPASSING

VROMM!

FOR MANY YEARS, HER ONLY COMPANIONS WERE THE DOGS SHE KEPT. THEY WERE OF MIXED AND GENERALLY ILL-TEMPERED BREEDS.

UNTIL ONE DAY, WHILE ON A NATURE HIKE, SHE HEARD A MOURNFUL CRY OFF TO THE SIDE OF THE ROAD.

THERE IN THE BRUSH WAS A BATTERED AND BLOODY MOUNTAIN CAT. IT HAD PROBABLY BEEN STRUCK BY A PASSING CAR.

WITH THE SAME STEELY RESOLVE THAT SHE BROUGHT TO GIVING HEPATITIS VACCINES TO SEX-OFFENDERS, SARA SCOOPED UP THE WOUNDED FELINE.

"MURDER, SORROW, SEX & REVENGE"

WHAT I LEARNED FROM MY GERBILS

"TALES OF MERE EXISTENCE" BY LEV

My brother was allergic to cats and we wanted a pet, so our Mom got us Gerbils.

We called them Skinny & Fats. We fed them and they had a running wheel.

We let them out of the cage to run around sometimes...

...and built them this real neat fort out of wooden blocks for them to play on.

One day our neighbor Jim Faden came over and kicked the fort down...

...and one of the larger blocks landed on Skinny.

My brother and I tried to wake Skinny up.

I took him downstairs & put him by the T.V.

If he doesn't move by the time Brady Bunch is over, he's dead.

We buried Skinny in the back yard, and used a brick for his tombstone.

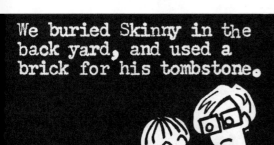

R.I.P.
SKINNY
1982 - 1983
KILLED BY
THAT DICKHEAD
JIM FADEN

Fats seemed lonely.

We bugged our Mom and got him a new friend, a girl we named Fatricia.

They got along fine.

Soon, Fatricia had seven pink hairless little babies.

Then they all grew hair and were really cute.

Then one day I was going to the cage to feed them...

...and saw that Fats and Fatricia had eaten three of their children.

Soon after that, the School Science Fair was coming up. I did my report on Gerbils...

SCIENCE FAIR
PROJECTS DUE
MAY 4

...because I was sick of my pets and wanted to get rid of them all.

FREE GERBILS!

It worked. All the kids wanted a Gerbil...

...so I didn't care about the grade I got.

Anyway, a week later, my teacher Mr. Holt called me to his desk and said:

The Gerbil you gave us bit my son.

I said I was sorry and told him I had not trained the Gerbils to attack.

But while I was walking away I was thinking...

...I really hoped the Gerbil would bite Mr. Holt too.

Ben Claassen

"They wanted me to be a nice housecat, but I just wanted to be feral!"

The Story of My Friend Jennifer & I,
And of the Important Matters in Our Lives.

→ SHE LIKED ME. AND VICE VERSA.

I HAD A HIGHSCHOOL FRIEND NAMED JENNIFER. SHE HAD BLOND HAIR + BIG BOOBS. I WAS GLAD THAT

Ya wanna go camping? Dad's taking the boat up the Delta!

JENNIFER BROUGHT HER PET "RAT-O" ALONG. SHE MADE A PLAY AREA FOR HIM TO STAY, JUST OUTSIDE OUR TENT.

*D'you ever want to be **naked** in **nature**?*

hee!

I dunno...

I say we strip down an' sing!

SHE HAD A LOT OF CRAZY, HEARTFELT IDEAS.

BUT BEING A RAT DO YOU THINK I'D REALLY STAY?

Now, on the count of three!

One!

Two!

Lark Pien

'CRACK!

huff huff

Oh, man! The neck broke but—

CRACK!

CRACK!

shit!

HUFF! HUFF!

Do it again!

What the **HELL** do you girls think you are doing!?

MIRACULOUSLY, RAT-O RETURNED TO OUR CAMPSITE, 2 DAYS LATER. HE STAYED BY JENNIFER FOR MANY LONG YEARS AFTER THAT.

Fred Einaudi

A few years ago I saw a painting by Damien Hirst—not a darling of the animal rights set, thanks to his fondness for displaying dissected sheep and cow carcasses preserved in formaldehyde—entitled "Do you know what I like about you?" It's a giant canvas covered with thick yellow paint and the tiny, trapped bodies of butterflies who were intentionally captured, and died, on the artwork while the gloss was still drying.

I think of this painting when considering our strange, confused, often misguided infatuation with animals. In many ways, it is their exoticness, their wildness, their non-humanness that draws us to love them—yet that is also the source of our predictable failure to protect them from our own frailties and misconceptions. Yeah, we dress up our schnauzers in Halloween costumes, we teach gorillas American Sign Language, we put rhinestone collars on panthers and pose them next to sports cars for magazine ads. But, really, isn't so much of this fascination with animals because they are, in their essence, *not* like us?

When we make dogs, cats, and other companion animals part of our families, we find that they often become subject to the same perversities we inflict upon our human relatives. In our society, we've more or less formalized ways to deal with child abusers, wife batterers, war criminals, and garden-variety sadists. But we're still figuring out what to do when our dysfunctions end up crushing the wild out of the animals we attempt to love or, more tragically, to control. At the Animal Legal Defense Fund, we hear such stories every day: cats doused in gasoline and lit on fire by "boys being boys," chimpanzees having the "smiles" beaten onto their faces for Hollywood appearances, tigers kept as house pets mauling their keepers (to whose surprise?).

afterword

We're grateful for *Pet Noir*'s efforts to depict the stories of our tender, abject, sad, and often downright bizarre relationships with animals. Maybe the first step in making the world a safer, more humane place for all of them—the snuggly puppies, the creepy crocodiles, the countless rats, gerbils, and other unwanteds euthanized in shelters every day—is to consider what a truly surreal state of affairs we've managed to create for them on this planet. To give it all a read, sit back, and really ponder, "What the cluck?"

Lisa Franzetta
Animal Legal Defense Fund
Cotati, California

Animal Legal
Defense Fund

Animal Legal Defense Fund

www.aldf.org (707) 795-2533

For more than a quarter-century, the Animal Legal Defense Fund has been fighting to protect the lives and advance the interests of animals through the legal system. Founded by attorneys active in shaping the emerging field of animal law, ALDF has blazed the trail for stronger enforcement of anti cruelty laws and more humane treatment of animals in every corner of American life. Today, ALDF's ground-breaking efforts to push the U.S. legal system to end the suffering of abused animals are supported by hundreds of dedicated attorneys and more than 100,000 members.

Animal Place

www.animalplace.org (707) 449-4814

Animal Place, founded in 1989, is a nonprofit sanctuary for abused and discarded farmed animals. Rescued individuals and indigenous wildlife share 60 acres of forest, meadow, pasture, hills, and a small lake. Animal Place is also a humane education center that works to promote cruelty-free lifestyles and veganism. They provide a variety of educational resources for both children and adults that teach kindness and compassion for all creatures and implement nationwide educational programs.

Animal Protection Institute

www.api4animals.org (916) 447-3085

Founded in 1968, API's mission is to advocate for the protection of animals from cruelty and exploitation. API's primary campaign areas currently include animals used in entertainment, captive exotic animals, companion animals, compassionate consumerism, farmed animals, and wildlife protection. API also provides "hands-on" care for animals at the API Primate Sanctuary, located in Dilley, Texas, where more than 400 primates, many of whom were rescued from abusive situations in laboratories, roadside zoos, and private possession, live in as natural an environment as possible with minimal human interference.

Best Friends

www.bestfriends.org (435) 644-2001

Best Friends is working to bring about a time when there are No More Homeless Pets. The sanctuary, at the heart of Southern Utah's Golden Circle of national parks, is home, on any given day, to about 1,500 dogs, cats, horses, rabbits, and other animals. Best Friends reaches across the nation, helping humane groups, individual people, and entire communities to set up spay/neuter, shelter, foster, and adoption programs in their own neighborhoods, cities, and states.

Farm Sanctuary

www.farmsanctuary.org   (607) 583-2225

Farm Sanctuary was founded in 1986 to combat the abuses of industrialized farming and to encourage a new awareness and understanding about "farm animals." At Farm Sanctuary, these animals are friends, not food. Over the years, they have rescued thousands of animals and educated millions of people about their plight. Farm Sanctuary also reaches out to legislators and businesses and works to bring about institutional reforms.

Humane Society of the United States

www.hsus.org (202) 452-1100

The Humane Society of the United States (HSUS) has worked since 1954 to promote the protection of all animals. They work to reduce suffering and to create meaningful social change for animals by advocating for public policies to protect animals, investigating cruelty and working to enforce existing laws, educating the public about the issues, and conducting hands-on programs, such as assisting animals when disasters strike. Their major campaigns target four primary issues: 1) factory farming, 2) animal fighting and other forms of animal cruelty, 3) the fur trade, and 4) inhumane sport hunting practices.

In Defense of Animals

www.indefenseofanimals.org (415) 388-9641

In Defense of Animals' campaigns and programs cover animals around the world, through investigation, rescue and rehabilitation, public education, political and consumer advocacy, and litigation. From working to protect the rights of America's companion animals, to rescuing feral goats on Catalina Island, to fighting to end the horrific trade in dog meat in Korea, IDA's campaigns reach far and wide.

National Anti-Vivisection Society

www.navs.org (312) 427-6065

The National Anti-Vivisection Society is a national, not-for-profit organization that promotes greater compassion, respect and justice for animals through educational programs based on respected ethical and scientific theory and supported by extensive documentation of the cruelty of vivisection. NAVS' educational programs are directed at increasing public awareness, identifying humane solutions to human problems, developing alternatives to the use of animals, and working with like-minded individuals and groups to help to end the suffering of animals.

People for the Ethical Treatment of Animals
www.peta.org (757) 622-7382

Founded in 1980, PETA is dedicated to establishing and protecting the rights of all animals. PETA focuses its attention on the four areas in which the largest numbers of animals suffer the most intensely for the longest periods of time: on factory farms, in laboratories, in the clothing trade, and in the entertainment industry. PETA works through public education, cruelty investigations, research, animal rescue, legislation, special events, celebrity involvement, and protest campaigns.

Petfinder
www.petfinder.com

Petfinder is an online, searchable database of animals that need homes. It is also a directory of more than 9,000 animal shelters and adoption organizations across the USA, Canada and Mexico. Petfinder's mission is to use internet technology and the resources it can generate to increase public awareness of the availability of high-quality adoptable pets and to increase the overall effectiveness of pet adoption programs across North America to the extent that the euthanasia of adoptable pets is eliminated.

Physicians Committee for Responsible Medicine
www.pcrm.org (202) 686-2210

Founded in 1985, the Physicians Committee for Responsible Medicine is a nonprofit organization that promotes preventive medicine, conducts clinical research, and encourages

higher standards for ethics and effectiveness in research. Supported by physicians and laypersons, they support the power of preventative medicine and good nutrition via healthful vegetarian diets, and they promote alternatives to animal research. PCRM has worked to put a stop to gruesome animal experiments, such as the military's cat-shooting studies, DEA narcotics experiments, and monkey self-mutilation projects.

Bitter Pie

about the artists

Alixopulos is a cartoonist from Northern California. His work has been published in Red Herring, East Bay Express and Legal Action comics, among other venues, including his own small press comic Quagga. His graphic novel, Mine Tonight, was just released by Portland-based Sparkplug Comic Book. His family had goats for a time when he was a boy and he sometimes milked Cotton and Cotton II.

Hailing from the planet earth, young **Andy Ristaino** was awarded the Anderson Lanbridge Fellowship in 2003, and has published such fine books as Life of a Fetus and The Babysitter, as well as being printed in numerous magazines, and anthologies such as the one you grasp in your fingers now. While he doesn't have a pet of his own, you can find him mixing it up with the likes of Sgt. Leon Tikis, Monster, Venom and sometimes Meowie MC Meow Meow. You can reach him via the interzone at *someone@skronked.com* or at *http://skronked.com*.

Artist **Ben Claassen III** is a regular illustrator for the Washington City Paper and is the creator of the weekly comic strip Dirt Farm. Over the last many years, he has taken care of several formerly living animals including a rabbit, a cat named Jimmy, some baby turtles, and a tarantula that lived inside of a really elaborate LEGO town. He has done illustrations for a number of publications, including actor Wil Wheaton's book of short stories, Dancing Barefoot. Ben's work can be seen at *bendependent.com* and *killoggs.com*.

Artist **Bitter Pie** is the creator of Bitter Pie Comix and Not Your Bitch printed productions. Her creations have been featured in hundreds of venues and festivals worldwide, including four independently funded book, CD, and record distribution tours across Europe. Throughout her life, each of her beloved pets (turtles, birds, cats, dogs, gerbils, mice, ants, frogs, and fish) have suffered horrible, tragic deaths. She no longer has pets. Find out more on her website *notyourbitch.net*.

"The Petaluma Cat Lady" and "The Freeway Incident" co-artist and layout friend **C.Ric Mose** has been drawing since before he can remember. Encouraged by his parents (both musicians) and friends, C.Ric began illustrating for a local newspaper while still in high school, and doing graphic design for family friends. Formerly educated in illustration at the California College of Arts and Crafts, he currently contributes to book covers and interiors, technical illustrations, community murals, and gallery showings. C.Ric lives with his iguana, Erasmus. His artwork can be viewed at *graphicilluminations.com*.

Damien Jay recently shipped his cats from Brooklyn, NY to Berkeley, CA. Weeks later, he joined them. He now spends his days regulating their access to the outdoors and the indoors, as well as working on his comics. See stuff like The Merpeople of Columbus, Ohio and Joey the Man-Cat at *damienjay.com*.

Eric Koepfle works in the scintillating field of technical analysis by day, and ventures into illustration by nightfall. With degrees in Anthropology/Archaeology and Fine Art, his master plan is a mystery to everyone including himself. Eric recently spent most of his waking hours drawing part one of the graphic novel *Fortune's Bitch*, written by Shannon O'Leary. During those long hours, he was incessantly pestered by his vociferous black cat Circe. She frequently crosses his path. *Fortunesbitch. com* and *prophet.net* are also his creations.

Eric Saxby studied biology at UC Berkeley, but then realized he didn't want to work in a lab for the rest of his life. Or ever. So he tried out some other careers. All along he wanted to create art and comics, though, and all along that's what actually made him happy, so now he works at an SF art gallery and is trying to produce more. Every time he's had a lucid dream, it's been triggered by a posthumous visit by an ex-cat. Check out *www.livingin-thepast.org*.

Fly lives with Bunny Blackjack in a former squat in the Lower East Side of Manhattan, where she paints, draws comics and illustrations, and sometimes paints murals. Her work has been published by NYPress, Juxtapoz, The Comics Journal and many more. Fly has self-published numerous comics and zines, including a collection entitled CHRON!IC!RIOTS!PA!SM!. PEOPs, a collection of portraits and stories, was published in 2003 by Soft Skull Press. Visit Fly's website at *bway.net/~fly* or email *fly@bway.com*.

An art school dropout, artist **Fred Einaudi** started painting again after realizing what a complete and total loser he had become. Fred likes pigeons. Email him at *feinaudi@yahoo.com*.

When **Janet Flemer** was eight, she saw the family dog, a sweet beagle named Bella, get hit by a car. Bella was fixed up by veterinarian/ Dad, but neither she nor Janet were ever the same. There are beagles living in her apartment building now, which makes her happy when it doesn't make her sad. Email Janet at *flemtown@pacbell.com*.

Artist **Jen Feinberg** has been drawing pretty much all her life. She has a BA from Rhode Island School of Design. Jen lives in Oakland, CA with Little Scrowlie writer Todd Meister and Little Scrowlie inspirational material/cats Hopey and Chi. Visit her website at *chi-jen.com*.

Artist **Joan Reilly** is a writer and illustrator living in Brooklyn, with her husband, a veterinarian. They share their home with 37 pounds of cat (that's three cats–Mister, Bessie, and Big Al–but Big Al takes up 23 of those pounds)

and nineteen pounds of dog (one slightly husky Jack Russell/Dachshund mix named Oly). For more information about Joan, visit her website at *hi-horse.com*, or write to her at *joanreilly@yahoo.com*.

John Isaacson has cared for dogs, cats, hamsters, rabbits, newts, snakes, horses, cows, and chickens. Sometimes he prints t-shirt designs of giant mutant cyborg half-human, half-animals from the future. In addition to self-publishing his mini-comic, Pyromania, his comics have appeared in Not My Small Diary, East Bay Express, and Sidewalk Bump. Look for his upcoming instructional graphic novel, Do-It-Yourself Screenprinting. You can see more of his work at *www.unlay.com*.

Lark Pien draws comics in her apartment in Oakland and paints in her studio in San Francisco. She is partial to animals who demonstrate naughty, haughty behavior. Rarely does she draw real life stories. For more of Lark's mostly imaginary terrarium, visit *www.larkpien.com* and *www.larkpien.blogspot.com*. For the record, though Lark is the creator of Long Tail Kitty, she does not own, nor has ever owned, a cat.

Lev is the creator of the ultra low budget comic and animation series Tales Of Mere Existence, based on gleefully embarrassing thoughts and stories from his own life. Films from the series have shown on Comedy Central's show Jump Cuts, as well as in innumerable festivals and has gathered a substantial cult audience on the Internet. Visit Lev's website at *www.ingredientx.com*. Lev has no pets, and truth be told, isn't too interested in acquiring any.

Layout wiz and graphic design geek **Lisa Thomson** enjoys drinking gin and tonics and spotting typos in menus. She lives in suburban bliss with her cat Buddy and her cattle dog mix, Sugar (a.k.a. "Concentrated Evil"). She spends much of her free time rescuing small animals from behind her bookshelf, and vacuuming up the balls of fur that roll like tumbleweed across her hardwood floors. Visit her at *lisathomson.com*.

"The Petaluma Cat Lady" artist **M. August Bournique** has no art education and a history of art exhibitions so scant as to be almost nonexistent. He comes to *Pet Noir* with a profound fear of pets and pet kitsch. He lives in San Francisco where he mostly paints cosmonauts, sells insurance, and maintains his large collection of oatmeal cable knit sweaters. Contact August by email at *h0b0king@yahoo.com*.

Artist, writer and *Pet Noir's* co-editor **MariNaomi** began creating comics in 1997 with her self-published Estrus Comics. Since then, her work has been seen in various publications, including Action Girl Comics, The Comics Journal, Not My Small Diary, and True Porn. She lives in San Francisco with her cat, Kitty, to whom she would like to dedicate her work on *Pet Noir*. Visit her at *marinaomi.com* or send her an email at *marinaomi@pobox.com*.

about the artists

Mary Fleener lives in southern California with her husband, a dog and two cats. She's the author of Life of the Party, and many comics. Her paintings have been shown at LA's La Luz and LACE galleries, and MoCA in Seattle, among other venues. Visit Mary at *www.maryfleener.com*.

Melanie Lewis lives in Berkeley with three cats and Damien, who is not a cat and is pretty helpful around the house. She used to have a yorkie named Lucy but said yorkie recently and unfortunately took a trip to "rainbow bridge", where she is waiting for Melanie to join her, according to literature from the vet. Melanie creates PS Comics, which contains stories of fruit and yorkshire terriers and mugs, but not all at the same time. See them at *pscomics.com*.

N8 Van Dyke never went to art school or anything close to it. Instead, he spent his time drawing in the back of his high school classes. N8's pissed off chimps have become well-known in San Francisco. Visit N8 at *n8vandyke.com* or email *n8vandyke@hotmail.com*.

Paul Musso's biggest artistic influences were traffic markings and instruction manual illustrations. His work has been published in numerous Bay Area journals, including Bananafish, H2SO4, Flatter!, and the Bay Guardian. He has a BA in art history. Paul's duck was killed by his older brother's dog.

Artist **Peter Conrad** has been displaying his artwork at galleries and coffee houses with an almost obsessive passion. His comics and zines have also appeared in the San Jose Museum of Art, and the Baltimore Museum of Art. Once, Peter saved a goat from drowning. Visit him at *peterconrad.com* and *attemptednotknown.com*.

Ric Carrasquillo is a story artist also unknown for his moody paintings. Ric has painted for a circus. He has ridden a camel and an elephant, but not a horse. Email Ric at *east_altus@mac.com* or visit *finishedline.blogspot.com*.

Scott Hewicker is an artist and musician. Sometimes his cat tells him to do bad things. He is represented by Jack Hanley Gallery and plays in the bands The Alps and Troll. Scott recently had his debut European exhibition at the Galleri Christina Wilson in Copenhagen.

Shannon O'Leary is currently working on a graphic novel with illustrator Eric Koepfle, entitled Fortune's Bitch. For info, go to *www.fortunesbitch.com*. Shannon also maintains a blog at *www.starryshine.net* for complicated reasons that involve another novel she is collaborating on and her love/hate relationship with celebrities. Email her at *shannonsplanet@yahoo.com*. She once had a three-legged cat who didn't like her very much. She lives in San Francisco with her dependable car, Steve-o.

acknowledgments

*P*et Noir could not have happened without the time, efforts, interest, and support of many good people and animals. Shannon O'Leary would like to thank Ajax Green, Mark Frischman, Christina Loff, Oren Kredo, Mark Pritchard, Brad Stark, Cory Vielma, Brian Musikoff, Heather Snider, Justin White, Julia Reischel, Lisa Franzetta, Roxanne Netaneneu, Lisa Thomson, Jennifer Joseph, Su Kao Merck, Amanda Fitzgerald, Xav Dubois, Shannon Klein, Bill Fitzsimmons, Jeff Stephenson, David Lasky, Cric Mose, Janet Flemer, Marcus Ewert, Kent Strader, Jesse Reklaw, Christine Shields, MariNaomi, Liz Walsh, Hal Looby, Suzanne Kleid, Josh Housh, Jess Baron, Eric Saxby, Jason Shiga, and everyone in the Tuesday art night crew.

She'd also like to thank the following bands for rockin' so hard on behalf of the *Pet Noir* cause: Ezee Tiger, Radius, Black Fiction, Fuckwolf, So So Many White Tigers, and Octomutt (along with rock impresario Jeff Ray of the Mission Creek Music Festival). And thanks to her incomparably amazing family, whom she loves very much.

Lark Pien would like to thank Jennifer and Rat-O for the good times. She'd also like to thank Dave, Solveig, Martin, Glenn, and Anna for being great with animals. She's learned a lot from you.

MariNaomi would like to acknowledge Lainie Baker, who was permanently scarred by Mari's cat. She would also like to acknowledge Kitty, the pussy who scarred her.

Melanie Lewis would like to thank Mosby, who sacrificed his cushy life in Virginia for her comic. She'd also like to thank all the other dogs on Rainbow Bridge, and Damien.

Peter Conrad would like to acknowledge Katie, the golden lab who modeled for the detective in "I Shoulda Known She'd Be Trouble."

acknowledgments

Scott Hewicker (and Shannon O'Leary) would like to thank Wayne Smith for all his help.

Eric Koepfle would like to thank his parents, his friends and coffee.

John Isaacson would like to thank his grandmother, Rosemary Laughlin, and his father, Deming Isaacson, for helping verify the facts of his story. He would also like to thank Shannon O'Leary, Mark Haven-Britt, Josh Frankel, Geoff Vasile, Jared Katz, Becca Criscillis and Jesse Reklaw for providing valuable feedback and criticism.

Lisa Thomson would like to thank her spoiled-rotten dog, Sugar, and her sociopathic cat, Buddy, for demonstrating just how far "cute" can take you in this world. She would also like to thank her recently departed cat, Pookie, for eleven years of friendship.